Reading Scales

All **measuring tools** use numbers and units to show the amount being measured. **Units** are standard measurements. They are shown as labels. For example, inches, cups, and pounds are units. Most measuring tools have **tick marks** (or small lines) between the numbers. The tick marks do not have numbers. Tick marks may stand for whole numbers or for fractions. Using the tick marks helps you make more accurate measurements.

Identify the amount represented by each tick mark.

1. 

____ pound

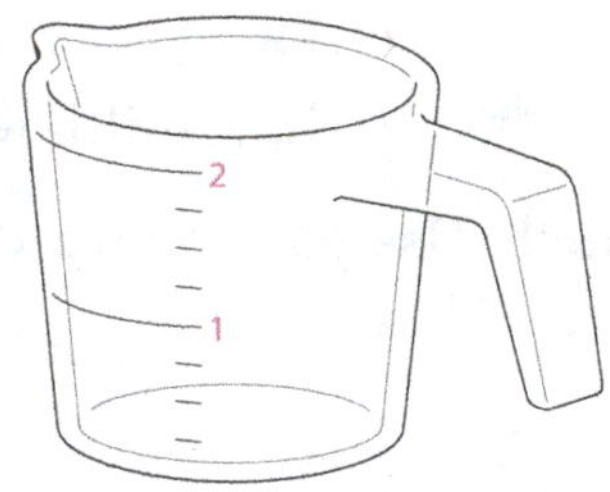

____ cup

____ °F

2. 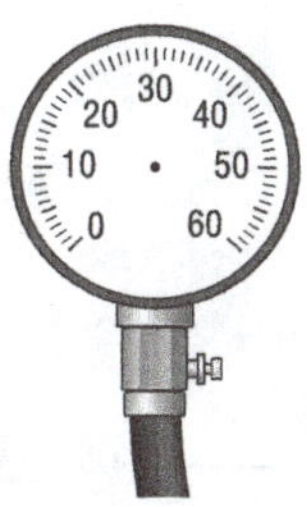

____ psi

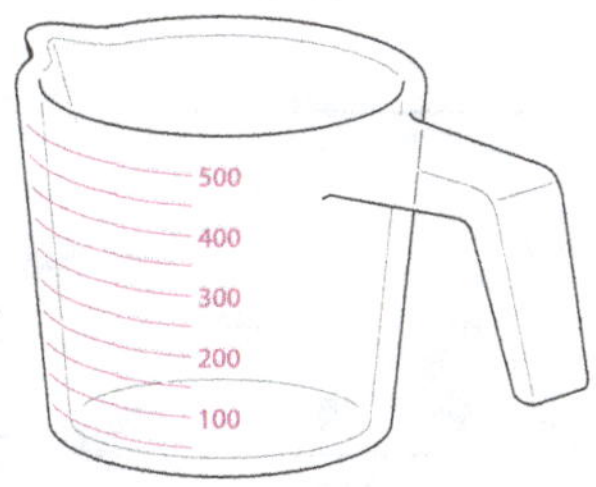

____ mL

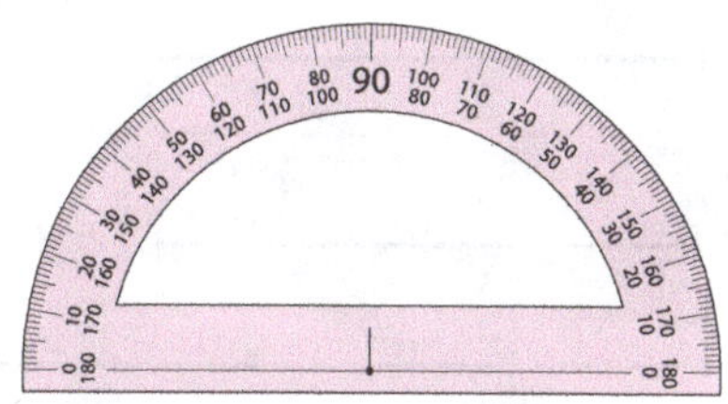

____ degree

Identify the amount represented by each tick mark. Then give the best estimate for the measurement indicated by the arrow.

3. 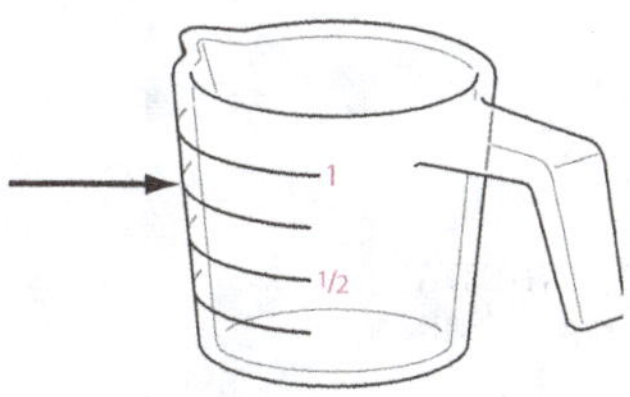

Tick mark represents ____________

Measurement reading ____________

5. 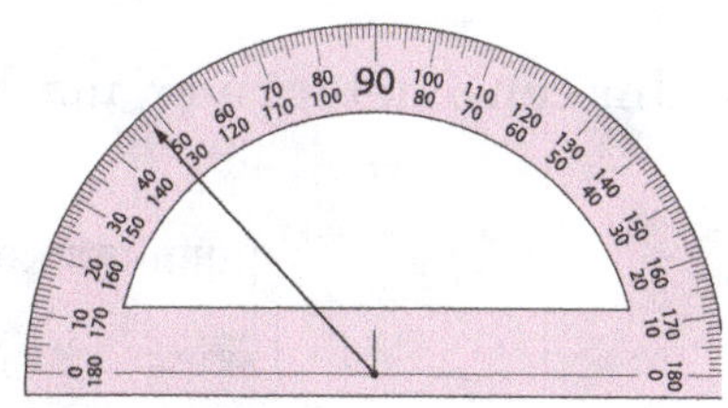

Tick mark represents ____________

Measurement reading ____________

4. 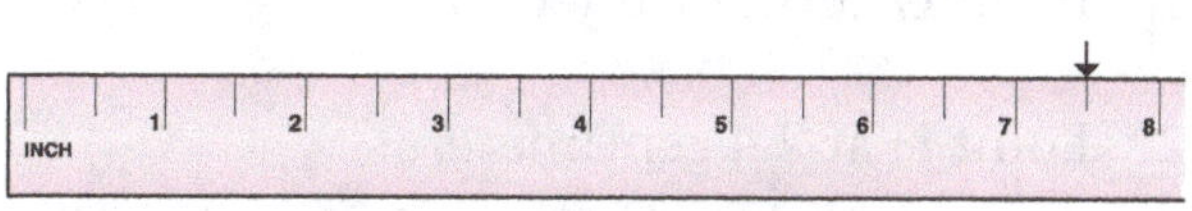

Tick mark represents ____________

Measurement reading ____________

6. 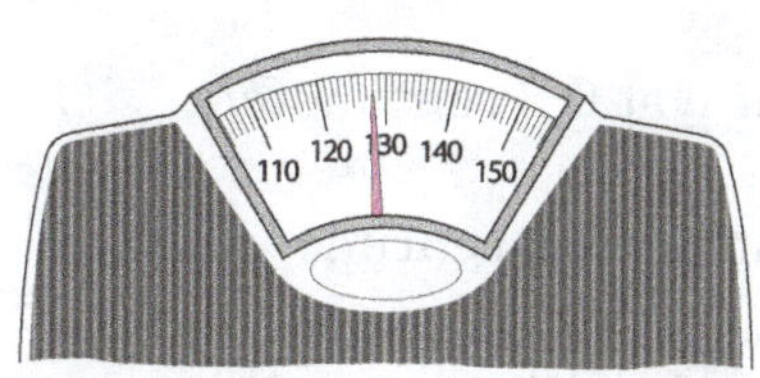

Tick mark represents ____________

Measurement reading ____________

Reading Rulers

Rulers are used to measure lengths.

inch ruler

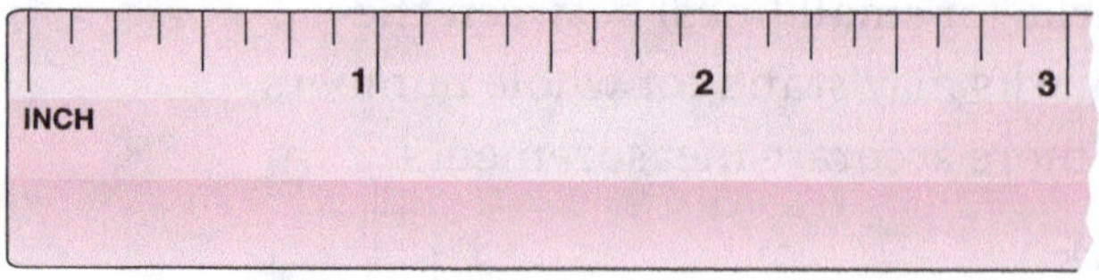

centimeter ruler

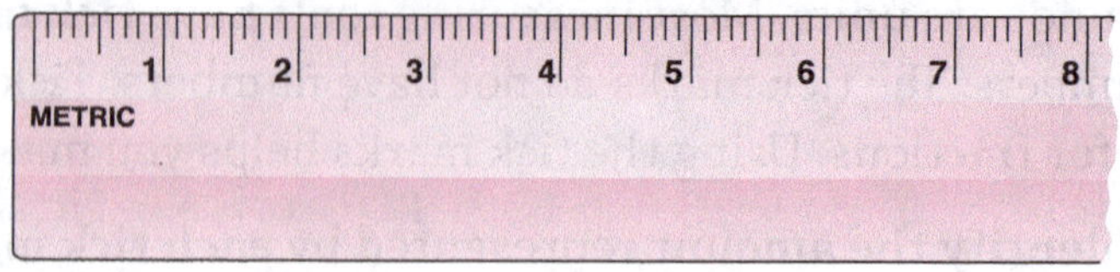

On rulers that measure inches, the marks between the inches usually show one-eighth, one-fourth, and one-half inches.

On rulers that measure centimeters, the marks between the centimeters show millimeters.

Measure each line to the nearest $\frac{1}{4}$ inch. Use your own ruler or trace a copy of the inch ruler onto another sheet of paper.

1. ______
2. ______
3. ______
4. ______

---

5. ______
6. ______
7. ______
8. ______
9. ______
10. ______
11. ______
12. ______
13. ______
14. ______

Above this centimeter ruler, mark the points.

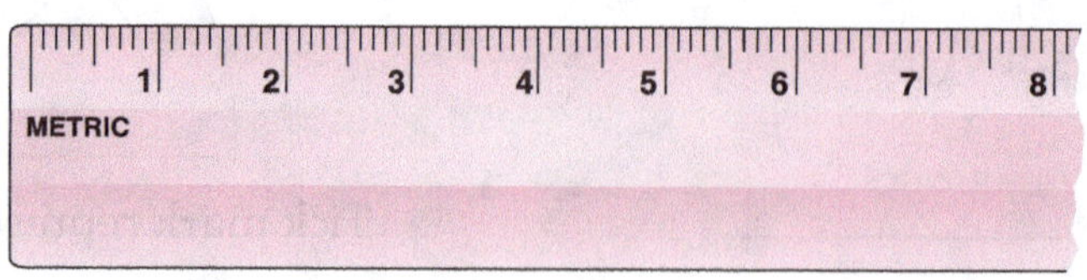

15. Point A at 3.5 centimeters
16. Point B at 0.3 centimeters
17. Point C at 7.8 centimeters
18. Point D at 1.5 centimeters
19. Point E at 5.2 centimeters
20. Point F at 0.7 centimeters
21. Point G at 6 centimeters
22. Point H at 2.4 centimeters
23. Point J at 0 centimeters
24. Point K at 4.5 centimeters

Customary Units of Measure

The units of measure commonly used in the United States are called **customary units.** Some measurements require a combination of units—for example, 8 pounds 4 ounces *or* 5 feet 4 inches.

Measurement Type	Examples of Customary Units
Length	inches, feet, yards, miles
Capacity	ounces, cups, pints, quarts, gallons
Weight	ounces, pounds, tons
Time	seconds, minutes, hours, days, weeks, months, years
Temperature	degrees Fahrenheit

On the line, write the customary units you would use to make these measurements. You may need to write more than one unit; for example, you might write *pounds and ounces*.

1. your height ____________
2. the length of a football field ____________
3. the temperature outside ____________
4. the weight of a bowling ball ____________
5. the capacity of a swimming pool ____________
6. the amount of time between presidential elections ____________
7. the weight of a cargo ship ____________
8. the distance between two towns ____________
9. the capacity of a glass of juice ____________
10. the point at which water freezes ____________
11. the weight of a suitcase ____________
12. the time it takes to cook a meal ____________
13. the capacity of a car's gas tank ____________
14. the weight of a small lizard ____________
15. the capacity of a coffee mug ____________

Choose the best estimate of the measure of each item.

10 ounces	35°F	1 gallon	2 pounds	104°F
1 ounce	4 months	10 yards	10 pounds	30 inches

16. ____________ temperature of a hot tub
17. ____________ amount of liquid in a drinking glass
18. ____________ weight of a grocery sack
19. ____________ width of a window
20. ____________ amount of fabric needed to make curtains
21. ____________ amount of liquid in a large milk jug
22. ____________ amount of time in a school semester
23. ____________ weight of three apples
24. ____________ weight of a wedding ring
25. ____________ temperature inside a refrigerator

Converting Customary Units of Measure

To convert, or change, from one customary unit to another (for example, from inches to feet), use multiplication or division. This table shows you some equivalent measures.

Length	12 in. = 1 ft.	3 ft. = 1 yd.	5,280 ft. = 1 mile	
Time	60 sec. = 1 min.	60 min. = 1 hr.	24 hr. = 1 day	7 days = 1 week
Weight	16 oz. = 1 lb.	2,000 lb. = 1 ton		
Capacity	8 fl. oz. = 1 c.	16 c. = 8 pt. = 4 qt. = 1 gal.		

Examples: How many pounds are equivalent to 35 ounces?
1 lb. = 16 oz.
35 ÷ 16 = 2 R3, so 35 oz. = 2 lb. 3 oz.

How many minutes are equivalent to 2 hours 40 minutes?
1 hr. = 60 min. 2 × 60 = 120
120 min. + 40 min. = 160 min.
so 2 hr. 40 min. = 160 min.

For each item, choose the equivalent measurement from the box.

256 ounces	2 pounds	336 hours	60 feet	1,320 feet
7.5 pounds	4 minutes	2 miles	3 pints	$2\frac{1}{4}$ hours
7 feet	2 yards			

1. 84 inches = ________ 14 days = ________ 16 pounds = ________ 6 cups = ________
2. 20 yards = ________ 32 ounces = ________ 135 minutes = ________ 72 inches = ________
3. 10,560 feet = ________ 120 ounces = ________ 240 seconds = ________ $\frac{1}{4}$ mile = ________

Convert each measurement. Write the equivalent measurement on the line.

4. 32 fluid ounces = ________ cups   12 pints = ________ quarts
5. 2 days = ________ hours   4 hours = ________ minutes
6. 61 yards = ________ feet   47 feet = ________ inches
7. 12 feet = ________ inches   96 inches = ________ feet
8. 17 pounds = ________ ounces   128 ounces = ________ pounds
9. 3 weeks = ________ days   8,400 seconds = ________ minutes
10. 4 quarts = ________ pints   112 cups = ________ quarts
11. 2 miles = ________ yards   1,760 yards = ________ mile
12. 8 hours = ________ seconds   654 minutes = ________ hours ________ minutes
13. 3.7 tons = ________ pounds   723 ounces = ________ pounds ________ ounces

Adding and Subtracting Measurements

You may need to regroup units when adding or subtracting units of measure.

Examples:

2 ft. 11 in. + 3 in. 2 ft. 14 in. = 3 ft. 2 in.	8 yr. 3 mo. = 7 yr. 15 mo. – 3 yr. 8 mo. = – 3 yr. 8 mo. 4 yr. 7 mo.

Solve these problems.

1.	5 ft. 7 in. + 6 ft. 8 in.	8 ft. 8 in. + 3 ft. 5 in.	4 min. 19 sec. + 9 min. 55 sec.	1 hr. 51 min. + 14 min.
2.	4 yr. 9 mo. + 9 yr. 5 mo.	13 gal. 3 qt. + 12 gal. 2 qt.	22 ft. 6 in. + 49 ft. 9 in.	6 yd. 2 ft. + 7 yd. 2 ft.
3.	28 lb. 8 oz. + 3 lb. 9 oz.	3 lb. 3 oz. + 1 lb. 13 oz.	5 yd. 1 ft. + 4 yd. 2 ft.	12 lb. 6 oz. + 41 lb. 12 oz.
4.	3 tons 1,500 lb. + 17 tons 500 lb.	18 c. 10 oz. + 14 c. 10 oz.	14 gal. 3 qt. + 45 gal. 3 qt.	6 min. 45 sec. + 15 min. 20 sec.
5.	13 ft. 9 in. – 12 ft. 5 in.	12 ft. – 2 in.	22 min. 8 sec. – 6 min. 15 sec.	4 hr. 30 min. – 3 hr. 47 min.
6.	9 ft. 2 in. – 4 in.	32 ft. 3 in. – 16 ft. 8 in.	3 gal. 4 qt. – 1 gal. 7 qt.	87 yr. 3 mo. – 39 yr. 6 mo.
7.	7 lb. – 3 lb. 10 oz.	35 hr. 8 min. – 12 hr. 35 min.	37 yd. – 1 ft.	11 tons – 750 lb.
8.	5 gal. 1 qt. – 3 qt.	62 qt. – 25 qt. 1 pt.	41 pt. – 19 pt. 1 c.	3 c. 4 fl. oz. – 1 c. 8 fl. oz.

Metric Units of Measure

Metric units are based on multiples of 10. The prefix of the unit identifies the place value of the measurement. To convert metric units, move the decimal point to the left when changing smaller units to larger units. Move the decimal point to the right when changing larger units to smaller units.

Examples: 1 g = 100 cg = 1,000 mg   1,000 mm = 100 cm = 1 m = 0.001 km

Meters (m) measure length.
Grams (g) measure mass or weight.
Liters (L) measure capacity.
Degrees Celsius (°C) measure temperature.

Metric Prefixes

milli- (m) is thousandths	deka- (dk) is tens
centi- (c) is hundredths	hecto- (h) is hundreds
deci- (d) is tenths	kilo- (k) is thousands

Circle the unit of measurement you would use to measure each item.

1.	distance between two cities	kilometer	meter	millimeter
2.	mass of a telephone book	gram	milligram	kilogram
3.	capacity of a can of soda	milliliter	kiloliter	liter
4.	length of a swimming pool	kilometer	centimeter	meter
5.	height of a first grader	millimeter	centimeter	kilometer
6.	mass of a postage stamp	kilogram	gram	milligram
7.	capacity of a water pitcher	liter	kiloliter	milliliter
8.	distance traveled on a bus ride	centimeter	kilometer	meter
9.	length of a baseball bat	centimeter	millimeter	kilometer
10.	capacity of a dose of medicine	liter	kiloliter	milliliter

Compare each pair of measurements. Use the symbols < (less than), > (greater than), or = (equal to).

11.	3 km ____ 30 m	1,500 mg ____ 1.5 g	32 m ____ 3,200 mm
12.	250 mL ____ 25 L	0.5 kg ____ 50 g	24 L ____ 2.4 kL
13.	5,000 cm ____ 5 m	500 g ____ 5 kg	72 kL ____ 7,200 mL
14.	34 mm ____ 0.034 m	7.8 km ____ 7,800 m	6.75 kg ____ 6,750 g
15.	4 m ____ 400 cm	13 mL ____ 1,300 L	68 g ____ 68,000 mg
16.	16 L ____ 160 mL	450 cm ____ 0.045 m	59,000 mg ____ 5.9 kg
17.	9 kL ____ 90 L	95 mm ____ 950 cm	5 L ____ 50 mL
18.	600 mm ____ 60 cm	75 kg ____ 7,500 g	32 km ____ 32,000 m

Time

Time can be divided in two groups of 12 hours—the A.M. hours and the P.M. hours. When calculating time, pay attention to A.M. and P.M. From 9:00 A.M. to 11:00 A.M. is two hours, but from 9:00 A.M. to 11:00 P.M. is 14 hours.

Read each problem and calculate the time.

1. It takes Melissa 30 minutes to get to work in the morning. She needs to be at work by 8:45 A.M. How late can she leave her house in the morning and still get to work on time?

2. Rusty is having a backyard BBQ. The coals take an hour to get hot. If he lights the grill at 2:30 P.M., what time can he start grilling?

3. Maryann works in an elementary school. She arrives at the school at 7:45 A.M. Her workday is 8 hours long. What time is Maryann ready to leave the school?

4. Alison is meeting a friend at his house at 7:00 P.M. Alison works until 5:30 P.M., and it takes her 1 hour to get home. Then Alison needs 10 minutes to get to her friend's house. How much time will she have at home before she has to leave?

5. Bernard goes to bed at 10:30 P.M. He is woken up four hours later by a car alarm. What time does the car alarm wake Bernard up?

6. Edda is flying to a business meeting. Her plane leaves at 12:45 P.M. She wants to be at the airport 2 hours before her plane is scheduled to leave. What time should Edda get to the airport?

Find the elapsed time in each problem.

7. Chris left for the supermarket at 2:30 P.M. He got back home at 3:15 P.M. How long was he gone?

8. Claire started to watch a movie at 8:30 P.M. The movie ended at 10:15 P.M. How long was the movie?

9. Luz put cookies in the oven at 4:35 P.M., and they were done baking at 4:54 P.M. How long did the cookies bake?

10. Troy started writing an essay at 7:15 P.M. and he finished at 9:37 P.M. How long did it take him to write the essay?

Points, Lines, Line Segments, and Rays

These terms and symbols are important in the study of geometry.

- A **point** • is an object that has a position in space. Use a capital letter to name a point.
- A **line** (⟷) is a series of connected points. A line extends forever in both directions. Use two capital letters (for two of the points connected by the line) to name a line.
- A **line segment** (—) has two endpoints and a straight path that connects those two endpoints. Use the two capital letters that identify the end points to name a line segment.
- A **ray** (⟶) has one endpoint, and it extends forever in the other direction. Use two capital letters to name a ray. The endpoint is always named first.

Write *point, line, line segment,* or *ray* on the line to identify the figure.

1.

______ ______ ______ ______

2.

______ ______ ______ ______

Draw each figure as directed.

3. Draw point *P*. Draw ray *QR*. Draw line segment *ST*. Draw line *XY*.

4. Draw $\overrightarrow{DE}$. Draw $\overline{OP}$. Draw $\overleftrightarrow{UV}$. Draw point *B*.

Use what you know about points, lines, line segments, and rays to answers these questions.

5. How many endpoints does a line segment have? ______

6. What is another way you can write "line segment *AB*"? ______

7. What is another way you can write "line *CD*"? ______

8. What is the endpoint in $\overrightarrow{FG}$? ______

Angles

Two rays that share an endpoint form an **angle**. The shared endpoint is called a **vertex**. An angle can be named by its vertex (for example, angle *M*). It can also be named by using three points on the rays that form the angle. When an angle is named by three letters, the vertex is the middle letter.

A **right angle** measures exactly 90°. An **obtuse angle** measures more than 90° but less than 180°. An **acute angle** measures less than 90°. A **straight angle** measures exactly 180°.

Identify each angle as *acute, obtuse, right,* or *straight*.

1.

_______ _______ _______ _______

2.

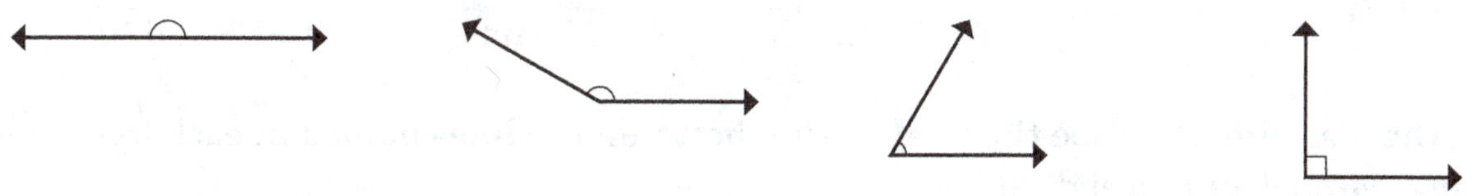

_______ _______ _______ _______

For each problem, use the circle's center as the vertex and draw the angle indicated.

3.

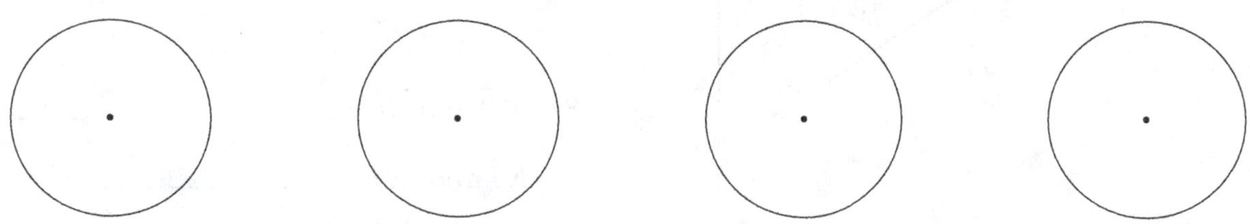

180° | 90° | acute angle | obtuse angle

Read each item. Then use the information given to name the points in the diagram.

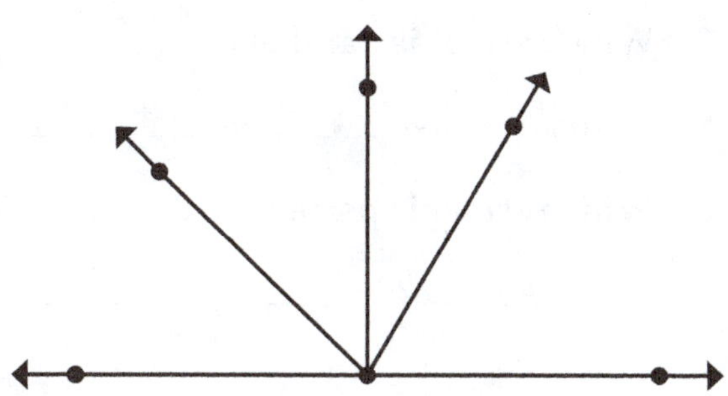

4. Label the vertex *C*.
5. Label the 180° angle *ACB*.
6. Find the ray that makes a 90° angle with $\overrightarrow{CB}$ and label it *CD*.
7. Find the ray that forms an acute angle with $\overrightarrow{CA}$ and name it *CE*.
8. Find the ray that forms an acute angle with $\overrightarrow{CB}$ and name it *CF*.

Lines

Lines that cross (or that will cross at some point) are **intersecting** lines. The point where the lines cross is called the **point of intersection**.

- Intersecting lines that form 90° angles at their point of intersection are **perpendicular**.
- Lines that will never intersect are **parallel**.

Use this figure to answer the questions.

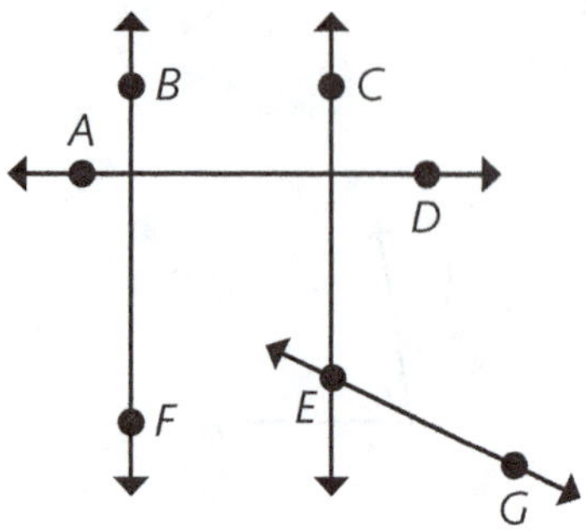

1. Which pair of lines is perpendicular?
   A $\overleftrightarrow{BF}$ and $\overleftrightarrow{CE}$ **B** $\overleftrightarrow{BF}$ and $\overleftrightarrow{GE}$ **C** $\overleftrightarrow{BF}$ and $\overleftrightarrow{AD}$

2. Which pair of lines is parallel?
   F $\overleftrightarrow{BF}$ and $\overleftrightarrow{CE}$ **G** $\overleftrightarrow{BF}$ and $\overleftrightarrow{GE}$ **H** $\overleftrightarrow{BF}$ and $\overleftrightarrow{AD}$

3. Which lines intersect at point E?
   A $\overleftrightarrow{BF}$ and $\overleftrightarrow{CE}$ **B** $\overleftrightarrow{BF}$ and $\overleftrightarrow{GE}$ **C** $\overleftrightarrow{CE}$ and $\overleftrightarrow{GE}$

4. Which lines will intersect if they are extended?
   F $\overleftrightarrow{BF}$ and $\overleftrightarrow{CE}$ **G** $\overleftrightarrow{BF}$ and $\overleftrightarrow{GE}$ **H** $\overleftrightarrow{CE}$ and $\overleftrightarrow{GE}$

Look at the diagram. Describe the relationship between the lines named in each item as *intersecting*, *parallel*, or *perpendicular*.

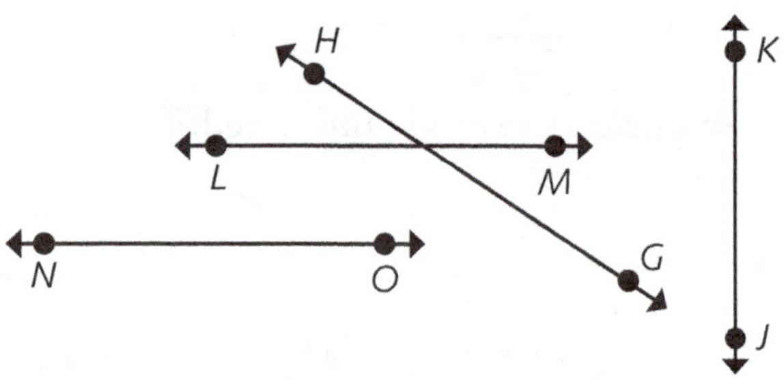

5. $\overleftrightarrow{LM}$ and $\overleftrightarrow{GH}$ ____________________
6. $\overleftrightarrow{LM}$ and $\overleftrightarrow{NO}$ ____________________
7. $\overleftrightarrow{LM}$ and $\overleftrightarrow{JK}$ ____________________
8. $\overleftrightarrow{NO}$ and $\overleftrightarrow{GH}$ ____________________
9. $\overleftrightarrow{KJ}$ and $\overleftrightarrow{ON}$ ____________________
10. $\overleftrightarrow{HG}$ and $\overleftrightarrow{KJ}$ ____________________

Study the map. Then answer the questions.

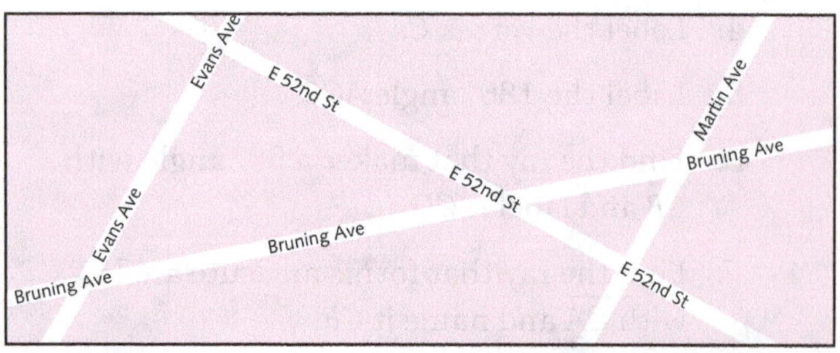

11. Which street is parallel to Evans Avenue? ____________________

12. Which street is perpendicular to Evans Avenue? ____________________

13. Which street, when it intersects Martin Avenue, forms right angles? ____________________

14. Which street intersects E 52nd Street, Evans Avenue, and Martin Avenue? ____________________

Polygons

Polygons are closed, flat shapes with straight sides. Polygons are named by the number of sides they have. **Regular polygons** have equal sides and equal angles.

triangle	3 sides	hexagon	6 sides
quadrilateral	4 sides	octagon	8 sides
pentagon	5 sides	decagon	10 sides

Cross out the figure in each item that is not a regular or irregular polygon.

1.

2.

3.
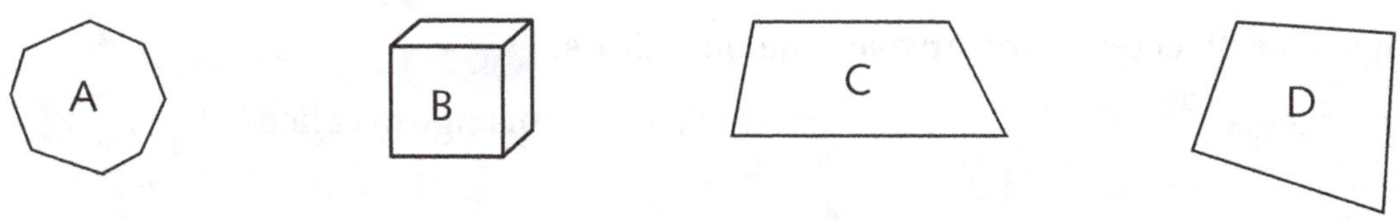

4.

Cross out the polygon that is not a regular polygon in each item.

5.
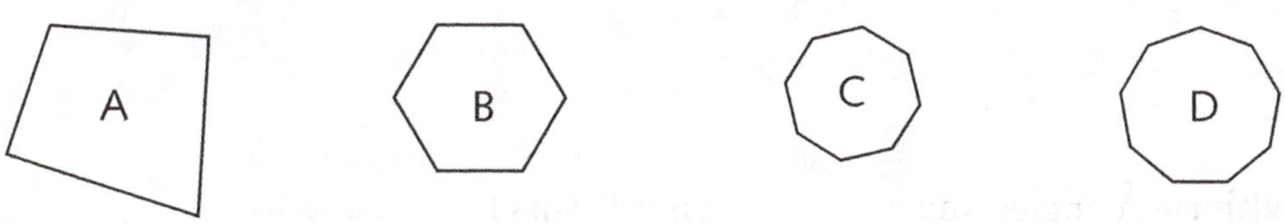

6.
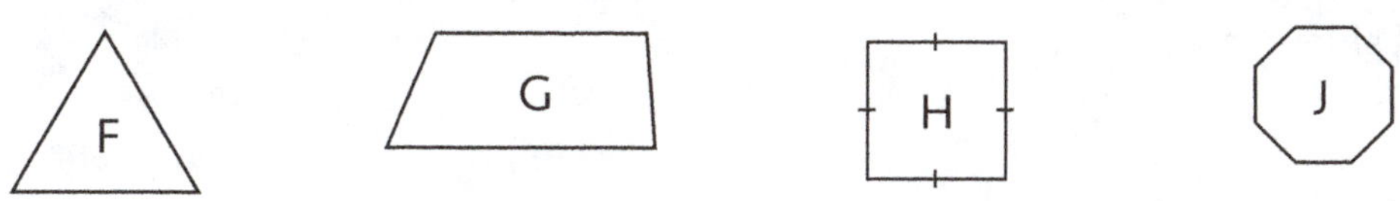

7.

8.

Special Quadrilaterals

Quadrilaterals are four-sided polygons.

- A **parallelogram** has opposite sides that are parallel and equal in length. Its opposite angles are equal.
  - A **rhombus** is a parallelogram with all sides equal in length.
  - A **rectangle** is a parallelogram with four right angles.
  - A **square** is a parallelogram with four equal sides and four right angles.
- A **trapezoid** has only one pair of parallel sides.

Choose the best answer for each question.

1. A square is a type of

   A rhombus
   B parallelogram
   C rectangle
   D all of the above

2. A rhombus is a type of

   F square
   G rectangle
   H parallelogram
   J trapezoid

3. A trapezoid is a type of

   A square
   B rectangle
   C parallelogram
   D quadrilateral

4. A parallelogram is a type of

   F square
   G rectangle
   H rhombus
   J quadrilateral

Draw each figure as directed. Then answer the questions.

5. a regular rectangle

   What is this figure called?

6. a parallelogram with acute and obtuse angles and all sides of equal length

   What is this figure called?

7. a parallelogram with right angles and two pairs of equal sides

   What is this figure called?

8. a quadrilateral with only two parallel sides

   What is this figure called?

Triangles

Triangles are three-sided polygons. They are identified by their sides and their angles. The sum of all the angles in a triangle is 180°. The sum of the length of any two sides of a triangle is always greater than the length of the third side.

Sides		**Angles**	
scalene triangle	three unequal sides	right triangle	one 90° angle
isosceles triangle	two equal sides (and angles)	obtuse triangle	one angle greater than 90°
equilateral triangle	three equal sides (and angles)	acute triangle	three angles less than 90°

Circle the correct name for each triangle. Tick marks indicate equal sides.

1\.

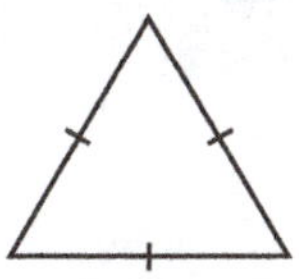

A scalene
B isosceles
C equilateral

A scalene
B isosceles
C equilateral

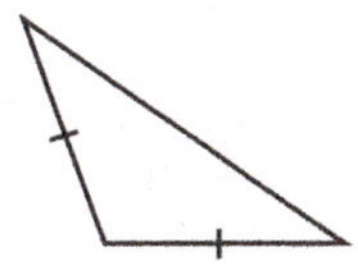

A scalene
B isosceles
C equilateral

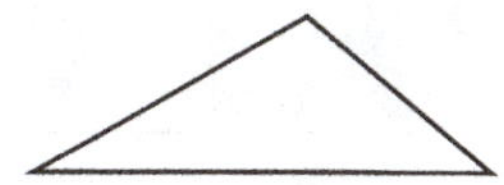

A scalene
B isosceles
C equilateral

Find the measure of the third angle in each triangle. Then name the triangle.

2\.

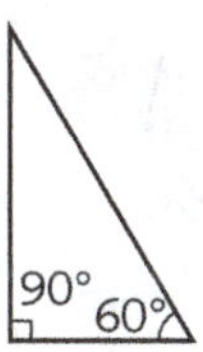

measure of missing angle ______

name triangle by angle ______

name triangle by side ______

4\.

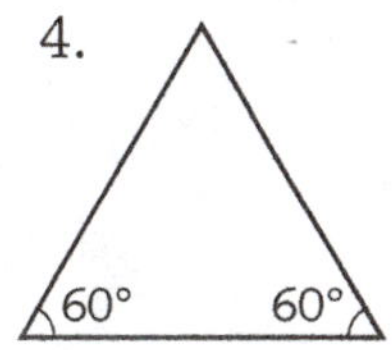

measure of missing angle ______

name triangle by angle ______

name triangle by side ______

3\.

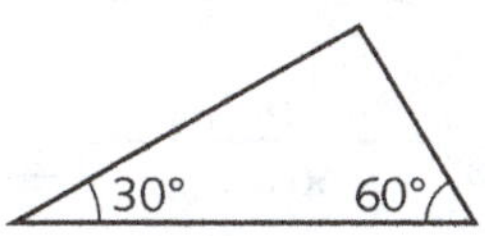

measure of missing angle ______

name triangle by angle ______

name triangle by side ______

5\.

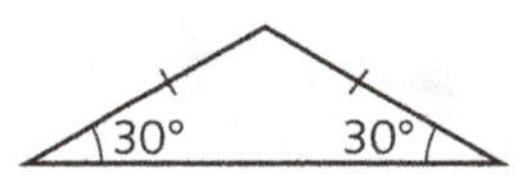

measure of missing angle ______

name triangle by angle ______

name triangle by side ______

Choose *T* for *true* or *F* for *false* for each statement.

6\. T F If two of the angles of a triangle measure 80° and 20°, the measurement of the third angle is 100°.

7\. T F One of the angles in a right triangle measures 30°. More information is needed to find the measure of the third angle.

8\. T F Every angle in an equilateral triangle measures 60°.

9\. T F A triangle could have sides that measure 3 inches, 3 inches, and 12 inches.

10\. T F An isosceles triangle with two angles that measure 20° each is an obtuse triangle.

11\. T F An isosceles triangle can also be an acute, obtuse, or right triangle.

Perimeter

Perimeter *(P)* is the distance around the outside of a closed figure. Add the measures of the sides of the figure together to find the perimeter. Use what you have learned about different figures to help you calculate perimeter.

- Regular figures have all equal sides.
- Parallelograms have two pairs of equal sides.
- Isosceles triangles have two equal sides.

Calculate the perimeter of each figure.

1.

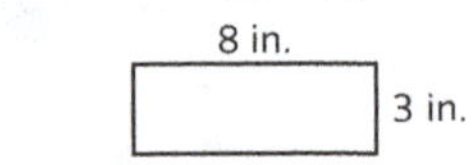

P = ________

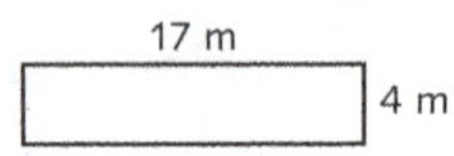

P = ________

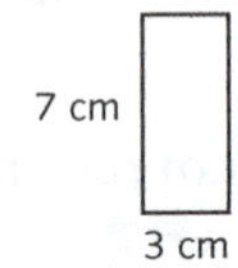

P = ________

2.

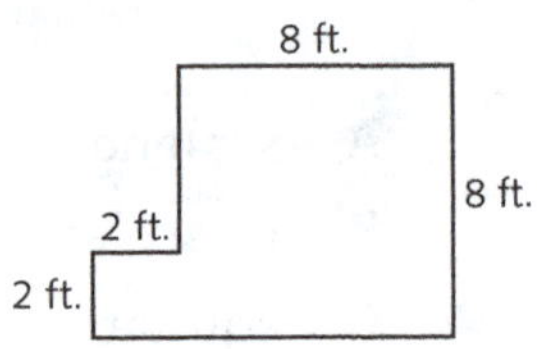

P = ________

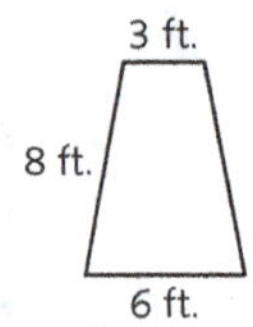

P = ________

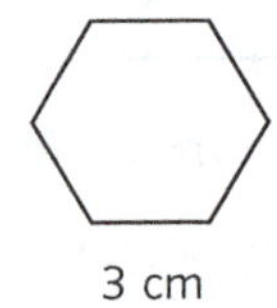

P = ________

3.

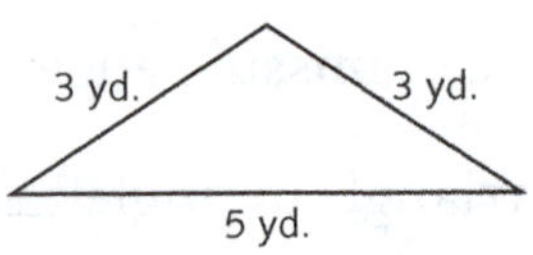

P = ________

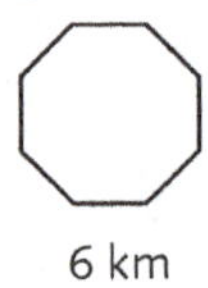

P = ________

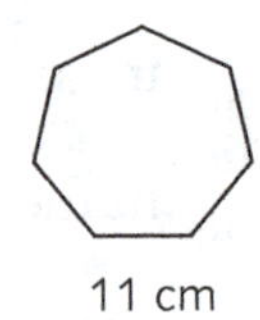

P = ________

4.

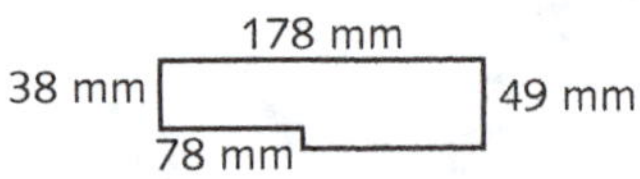

P = ________

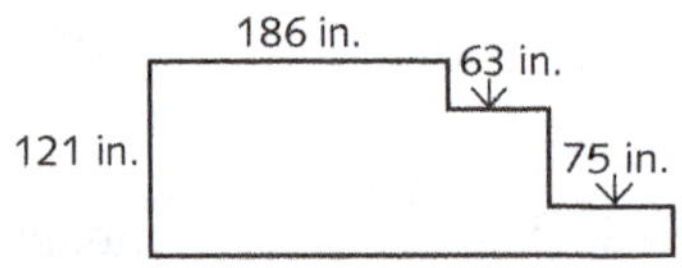

P = ________

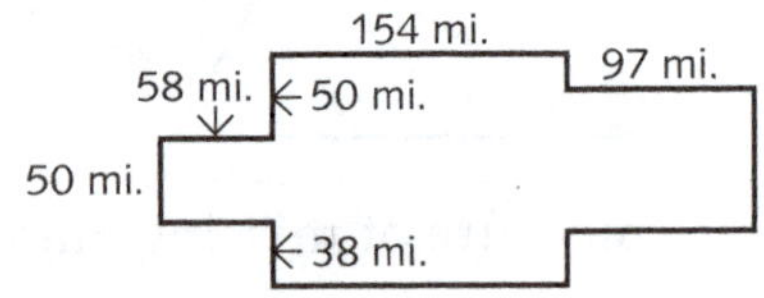

P = ________

Solve these problems. You may find it helpful to sketch and label each figure on a separate sheet of paper.

5. The perimeter of a rectangle is 46 meters. The long side measures 14 meters. What does each shorter side measure?

6. The perimeter of a regular hexagon is 36 inches. What is the length of each side?

7. The perimeter of a square is 48 feet. How long is each side?

8. The perimeter of a parallelogram is 124 cm. The sum of two opposite sides is 60 cm. What are the measurements of each side?

Area

Area *(A)* is the measure of the space inside a figure. It is measured in square units. Find the area of a rectangle by multiplying length by width ($l \times w$). A square has equal sides, so the length and width are the same. If a shape is made up of two or more rectangles, find the area of each rectangle and add the areas together.

Examples: $l \times w$ = 6 in. × 7 in. = 42 sq. in. $l \times w$ = 9 mm × 4 mm = 36 mm^2

Find the area of each figure.

1. 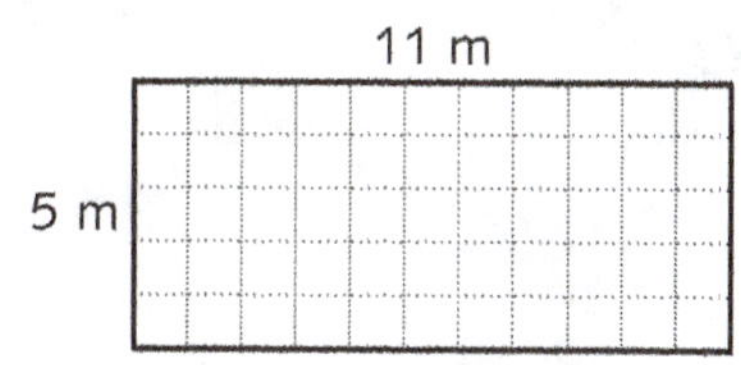

A = ______

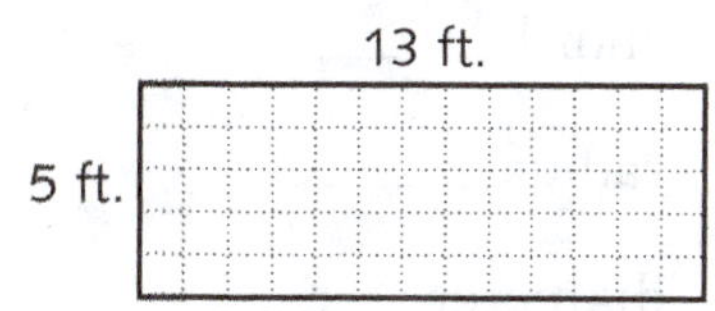

A = ______

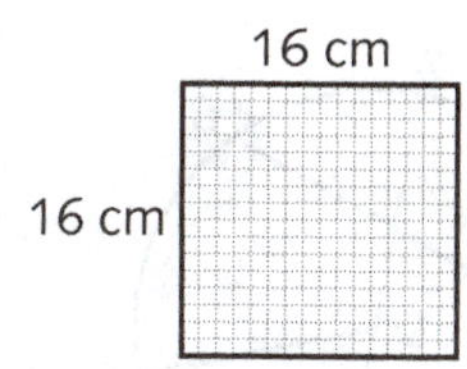

A = ______

2. 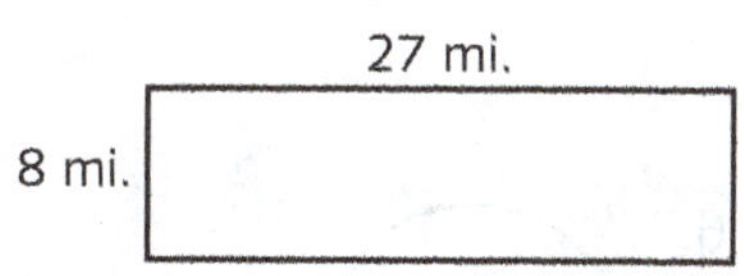

A = ______

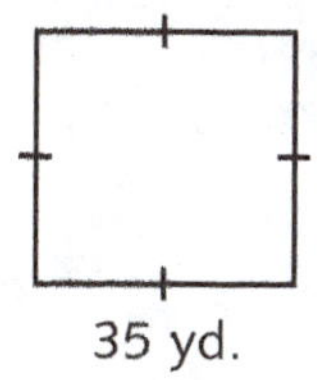

A = ______

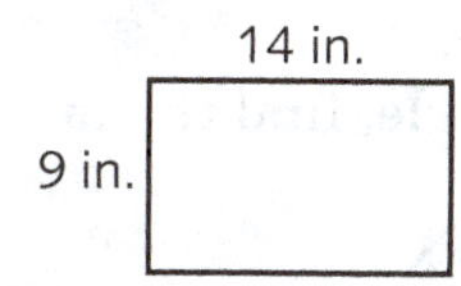

A = ______

3. 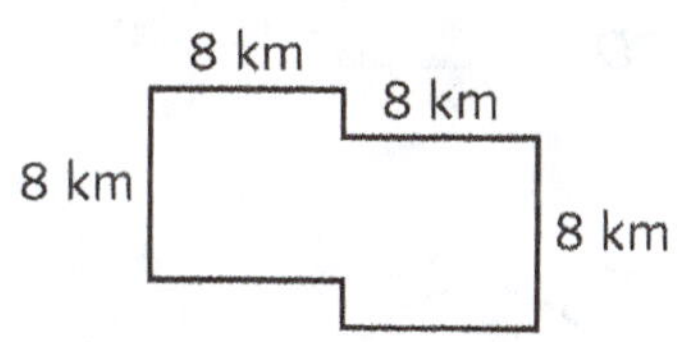

A = ______

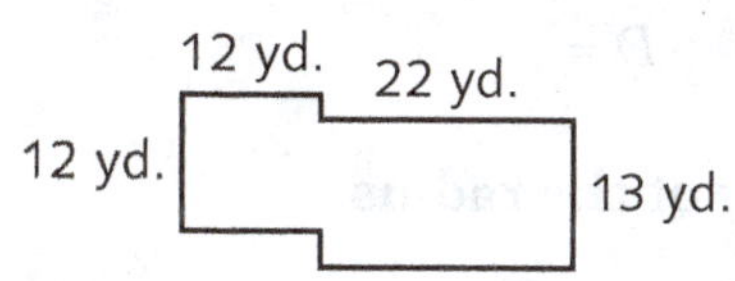

A = ______

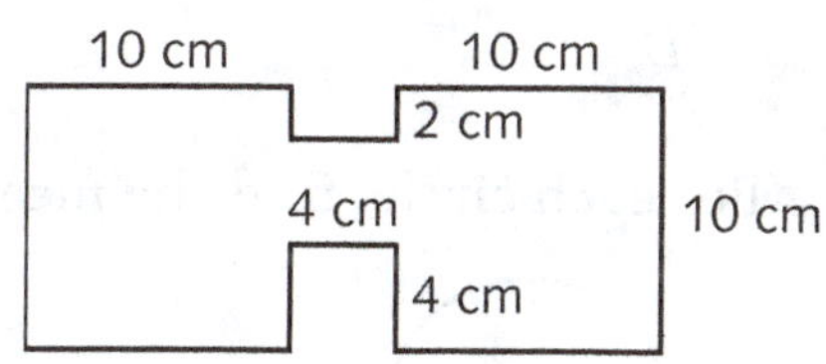

A = ______

Solve these problems. You may find it helpful to sketch and label each figure.

4. What is the area of a playground that is 16 feet wide by 20 feet long?

5. The area of a garden is 144 square feet. If the garden is 12 feet wide, how long is the garden?

6. Sue's bedroom is a square with sides that are 16 feet long. What is the area of this room?

7. Matt works on a desk that measures 36 inches by 48 inches and a table that measures 24 inches by 36 inches. What is the area of Matt's workspace?

Parts of a Circle

A **circle** is a set of points that are all the same distance from a given point called the center. The **radius** of a circle is a line segment from the center to any point on the circle. The **diameter** of a circle is a line segment that passes through the center and has endpoints on the circle. The diameter is always twice as long as the radius. A **chord** is a line segment that connects any two points on the circle.

Use the diagram to identify the part of a circle indicated.

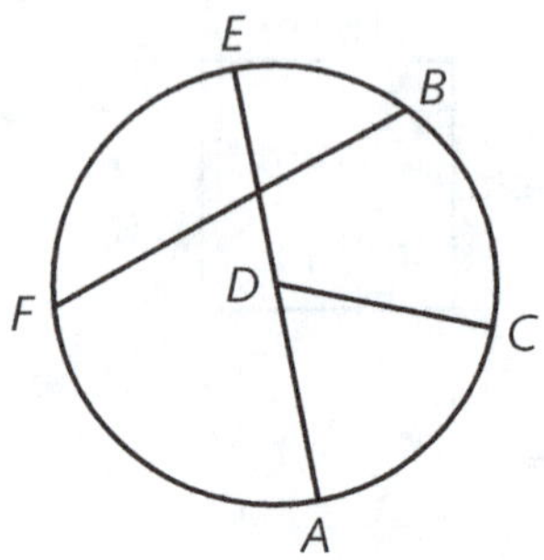

1. chord ________
2. radius ________
3. diameter ________

For each circle, find the measure of the diameter.

4. 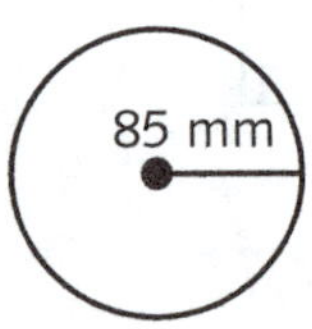

$D =$ ________

5. 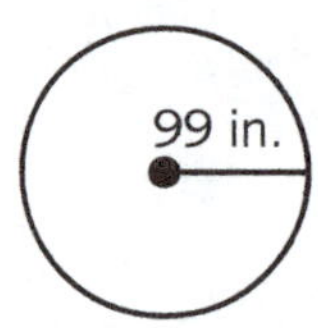

$D =$ ________

6. 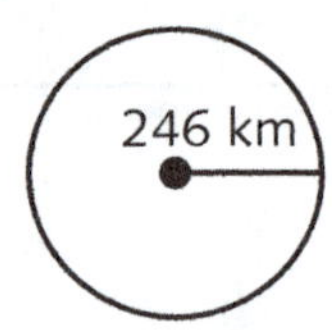

$D =$ ________

For each circle, find the measure of the radius.

7. 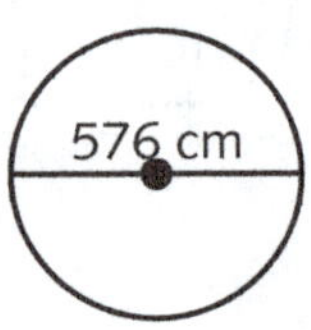

$R =$ ________

8. 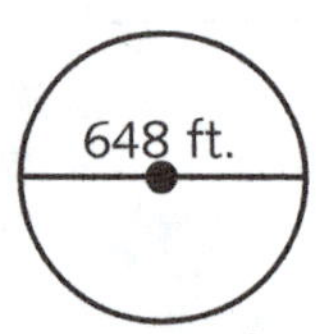

$R =$ ________

9. 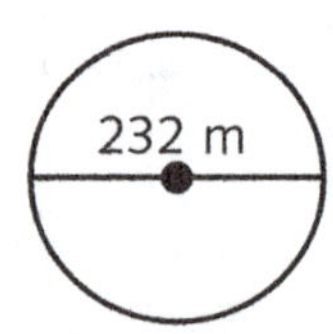

$R =$ ________

Use the circle to draw each item as indicated.

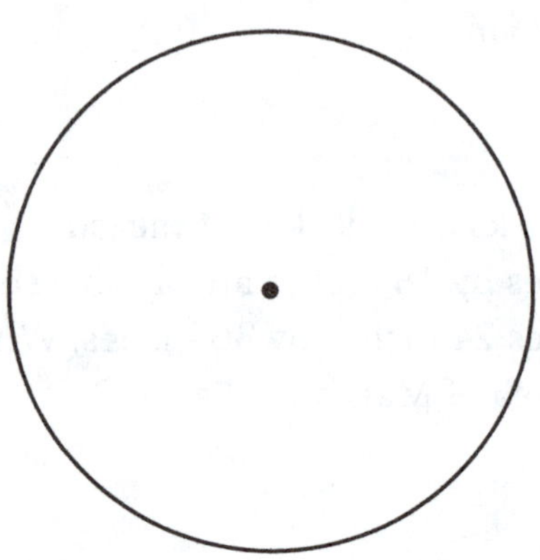

10. Draw radius *AB*.
11. Draw diameter *CD*.
12. Draw chord *FG*.

Visualizing Shapes

Being able to visualize shapes is an important geometry skill. Sometimes you can see only part of a shape, but you need to visualize the entire shape. At other times you see a whole shape, but you need to figure out how the shape can be split into smaller parts.

Look at each figure. Imagine that you are going to trace around the bottom of it. Name the shape that you would draw.

1. 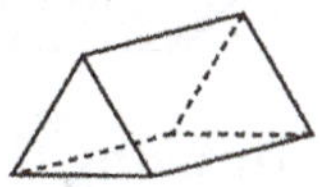  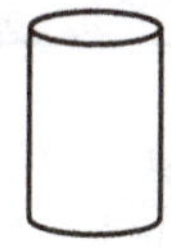

_______________ _______________ _______________

2. 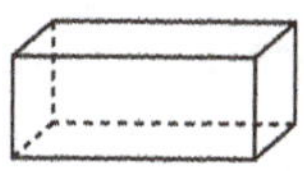 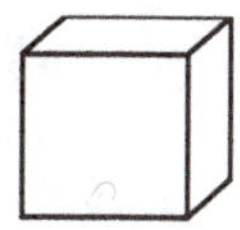 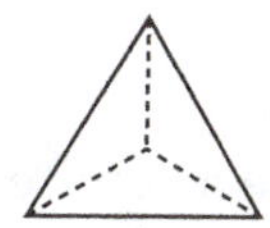

_______________ _______________ _______________

The first drawing in each question shows a piece of paper that has been folded in half and then cut. Choose the shape that would be the cutout when the paper is unfolded.

3. 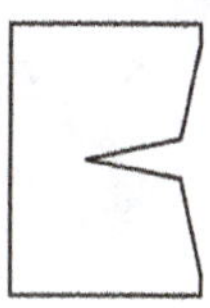

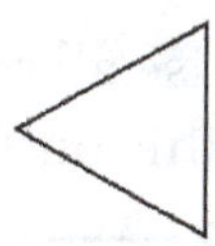
A

B

C

4. 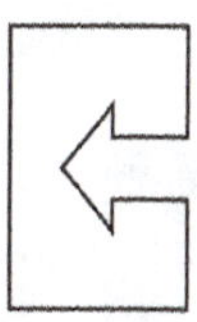

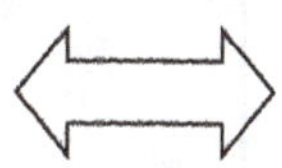
F

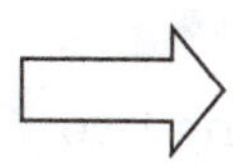
G

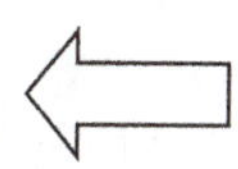
H

The first drawing has been folded in half. Choose what the figure would look like unfolded.

5. 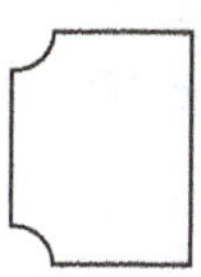

A

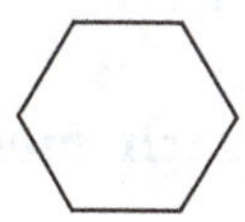
B

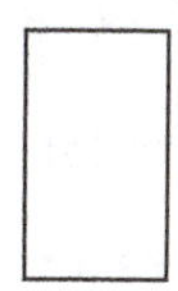
C

6. 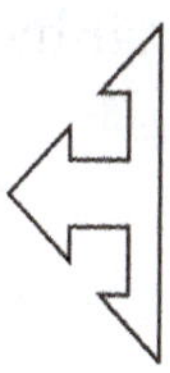

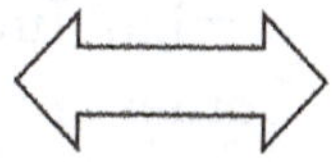
F

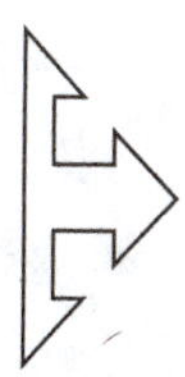
G

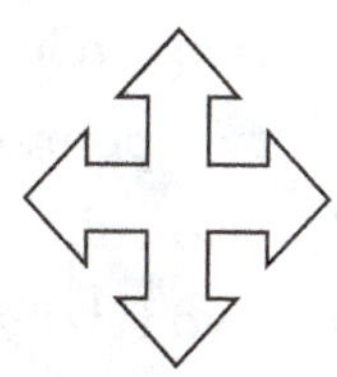
H

Visualizing Shapes

Trace these figures on a piece of paper. Next, cut the figures out. Then use the cut-out figures to solve these problems. Draw your shapes beside the questions.

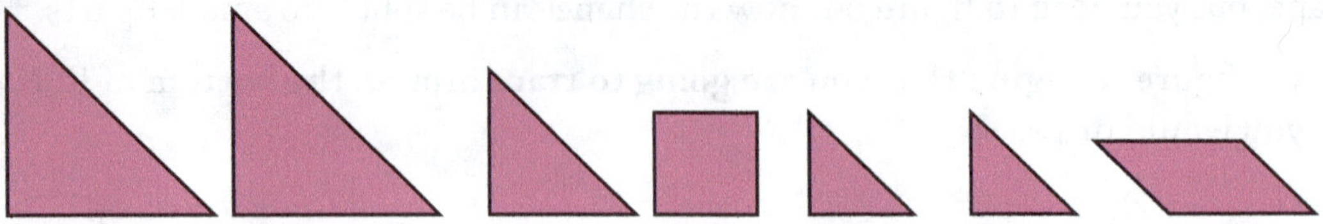

1. Make a square by using the two large triangles.

2. Make a square by using one medium triangle and two small triangles.

3. Make a square by using a large triangle, a medium triangle, and two small triangles.

4. Make a parallelogram by using two triangles and one square.

5. Make a trapezoid by using three of the shapes.

6. Make a quadrilateral by using three triangles.

7. Use all seven shapes to make a square. This outline will help you.

Circle the letter that answers each question.

8. Picture a rectangle that is cut in half from one corner to the opposite corner. What two new figures are made from this?
   - **A** two circles
   - **B** two pentagons
   - **C** two cubes
   - **D** two triangles

9. Picture a five-pointed star. What figure will be made if you connect each point on the star to the one next to it by using straight line segments so the star has a border around it?
   - **F** pentagon
   - **G** hexagon
   - **H** octagon
   - **J** pyramid

Symmetry

Some figures can be divided into two parts that look alike but are facing opposite directions. Each part is a mirror image of the other part. The dividing line between the two mirror images is called the **line of symmetry**. A figure may have no lines of symmetry, one line of symmetry, or more than one line of symmetry.

Circle the letter of the figures that have been divided by a line of symmetry.

1. 

A B C D

2. 

A B C D

3. 

A B C D

Look at each figure. Draw a dotted line to show the line(s) of symmetry. If no line of symmetry can be drawn, write *none* below the figure.

4. 

5. 

On the line below each figure, identify how many lines of symmetry the figure has. Write *none, one,* or *more than one.*

6. 

______ ______ ______ ______

7. **X** **B** **S** **N**

______ ______ ______ ______

Congruent and Similar Figures

Figures that are the same size and the same shape are **congruent**. Figures that have the same shape but not the same size are **similar**. Figures do not have to be facing the same direction to be congruent or similar.

Look at the first figure in each row. Then compare that figure with the other figures in the row. Write *congruent, similar,* or *unlike* below those figures.

1. 

______ ______ ______

2. 

______ ______ ______

3. 

______ ______ ______

4. 

______ ______ ______

5. 

______ ______ ______

6. 

______ ______ ______

Study the figure. Then answer the questions.

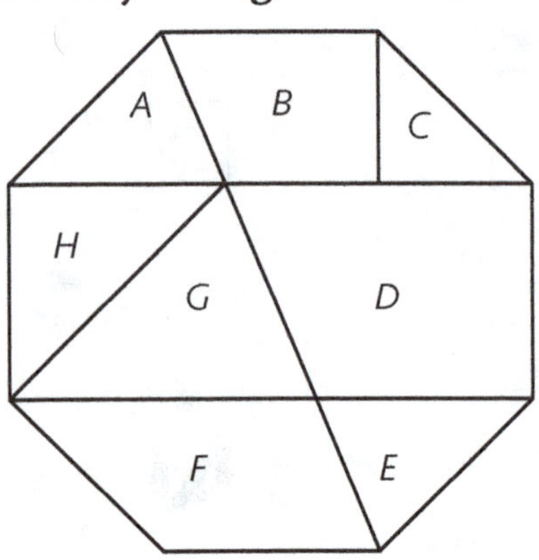

7. Which figure is similar to figure *C*?

______

8. Which figure is congruent to figure *E*?

______

9. Which figure is similar to figure *D*?

______

10. Are figures *F* and *G* similar, congruent, or unlike? ______

Three-Dimensional Figures

A three-dimensional figure, or **solid figure**, has length, width, and height (or depth). Each surface of a solid figure is called a **face**.

To find the surface area of a solid figure, find the area of each face. Then add those areas to find the total surface area.

Study each figure and identify the number of faces it has.

1. 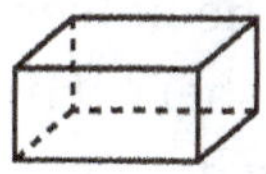

   ______

2. 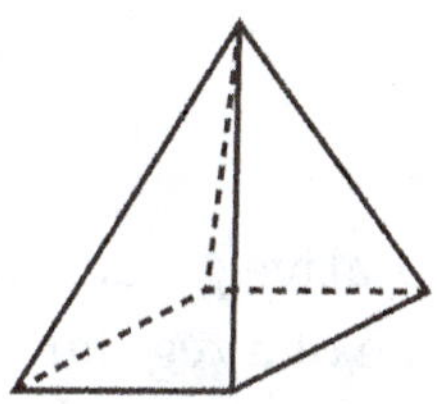

   ______

3. 

   ______

4. 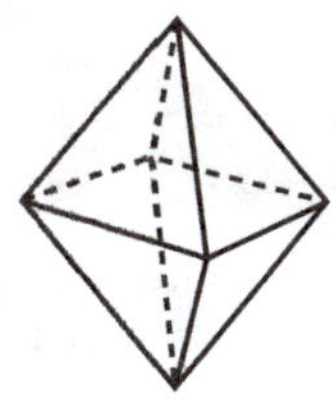

   ______

5. 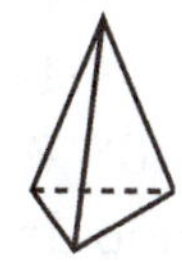

   ______

6. 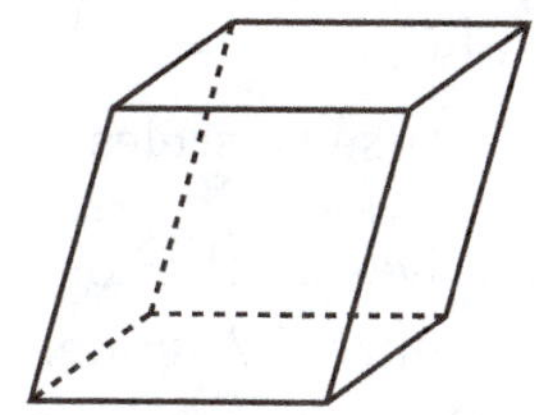

   ______

Find the surface area of each solid figure.

7. 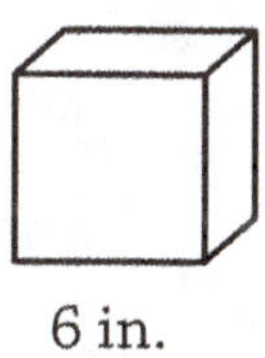

   ______

   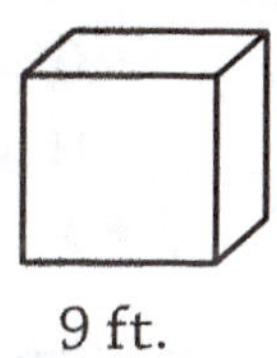

   ______

   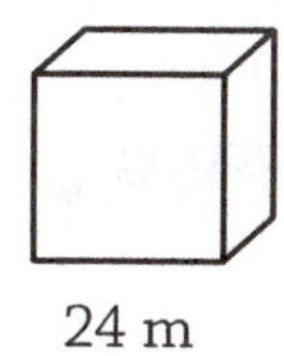

   ______

8. 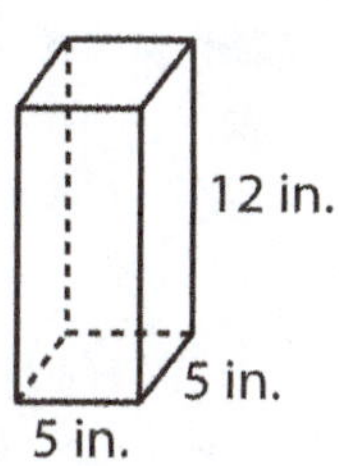

   ______

   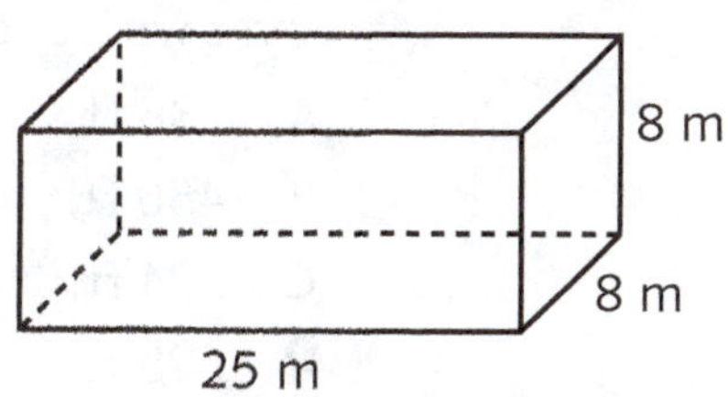

   ______

   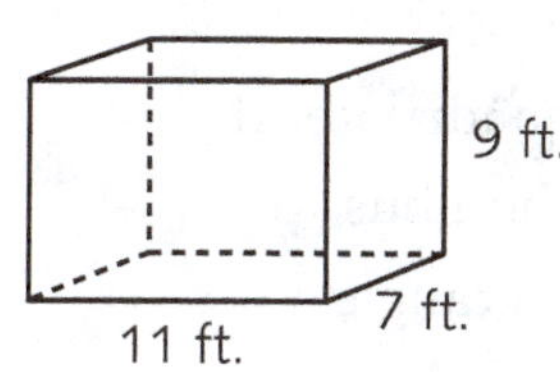

   ______

Name two objects described by each of these shapes.

9. cylinder ______________________

   ____

10. rectangular solid ______________________

    ____

11. cube ______________________

    ____

12. cone ______________________

    ____

Using Geometry to Solve Problems

You can use what you know about geometry to solve problems.

Choose the best answer to each question.

1. Raymondo is an architect. He is making two-dimensional drawings of a new house for one of his clients. He sketches the roof as a triangle with two equal sides. The angle between the sides measures 140°. What type of triangle did Raymondo draw?

   A right scalene
   B right isosceles
   C obtuse scalene
   D obtuse isosceles

2. Fiona lives on the corner of Dexter Street and Primrose Avenue. When the two streets cross each other, all the angles are right angles. What kind of lines are formed by this intersection?

   F parallel
   G perpendicular
   H intersecting
   J curved

3. Jin is drawing a figure that has four sides. Two of the sides are parallel but not equal in length. What shape has Jin drawn?

   A quadrilateral
   B rhombus
   C rectangle
   D trapezoid

4. The courtyard of a building is shaped like a circle. The blueprints show that the diameter of the courtyard is 87 feet. What is the radius of the courtyard?

   F 174 ft.
   G 130.5 ft.
   H 43.5 ft.
   J 21.75 ft

5. Flavia is cutting party decorations out of 8-inch-by-11-inch sheets of construction paper. How many different ways can she fold each sheet so that the halves are mirror images of each other? (Hint: How many lines of symmetry does each sheet of paper have?)

   A none
   B one
   C two
   D three

6. Rena is making a decorative garden bed in her yard in the shape of a regular hexagon. Each side is 3 feet long. She wants to put a wooden frame around the bed. How much wood will she need?

   F 15 ft.
   G 18 ft.
   H 21 ft.
   J 27 ft.

7. The Joneses want to buy sod for their backyard. Their yard is 25 feet long by 18 feet wide. What is the area they must cover with sod?

   A 36 $ft.^2$
   B 450 $ft.^2$
   C 324 $ft.^2$
   D 625 $ft.^2$

8. Brian has a cylinder-shaped object. If he places the object on a piece of paper and traces around the bottom, what shape will he draw?

   F circle
   G triangle
   H square
   J hexagon

Review

Study the figure. Do Numbers 1 through 3.

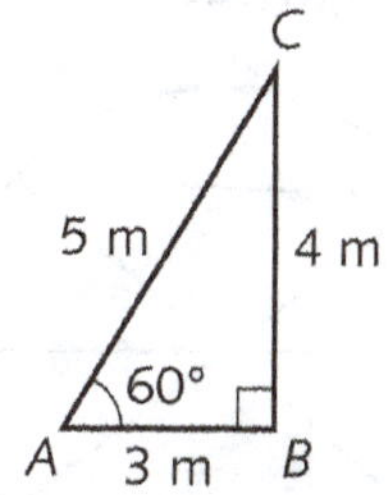

1 What kind of triangle is this?

A right
B acute
C obtuse
D isosceles

2 What is the perimeter of this triangle?

F 60 m
G 12 m
H 17 m
J 19 m

3 If ∠*A* measures 60°, then what does ∠*C* measure?

A 30°
B 60°
C 90°
D 180°

4 Tomas shipped two large crates. The first weighed 117 pounds 7 ounces and the second weighed 55 pounds 11 ounces. What is the difference in weight between the two crates?

F 52 lb. 4 oz.
G 168 lb. 2 oz.
H 61 lb. 12 oz.
J 167 lb. 18 oz.

5 Look at the time shown on the clock. What time will it be 30 minutes later?

A 3:20 **C** 4:20
B 3:30 **D** 4:30

6 Which pair of figures is congruent?

F

G
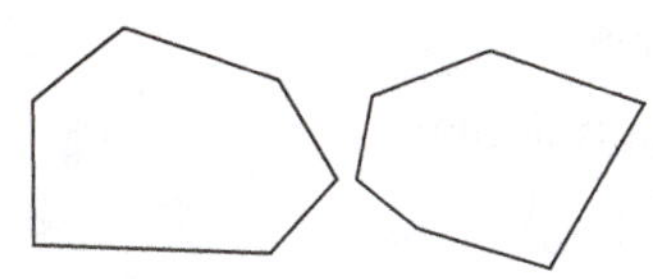

H
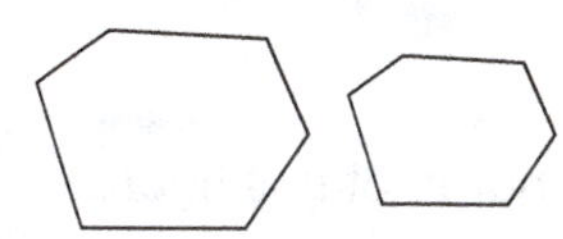

J
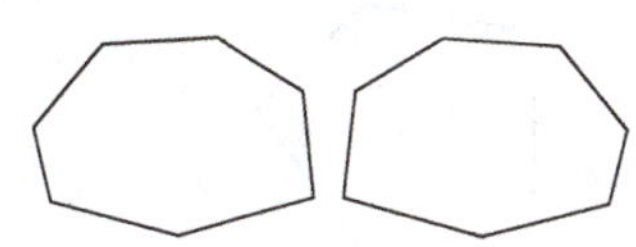

7 What is the best unit of measure for a bag of frozen blueberries?

A ton **C** yard
B ounce **D** gallon

8 How should this angle be named?

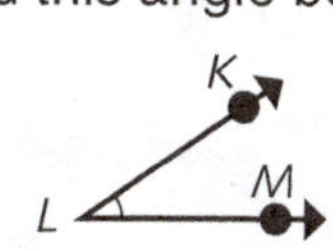

F ∠*KL* **H** ∠*LMK*
G ∠*MLK* **J** ∠*MKL*

Review

9 Which terms correctly describe these shapes?

A similar and congruent

B similar but not congruent

C congruent but not similar

D neither similar nor congruent

10 Which term best describes these lines?

F intersecting

G obtuse

H perpendicular

J parallel

11 What is the name of this figure?

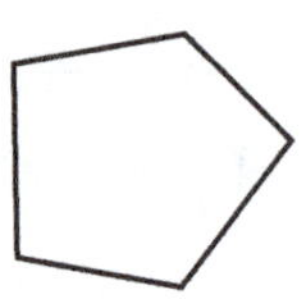

A quadrilateral

B pentagon

C hexagon

D octagon

12 What is the area of a square whose sides measure 17 cm?

F 136 cm^2

G 249 cm^2

H 289 cm^2

J 919 cm^2

Look at the figure and then do Numbers 13 through 16.

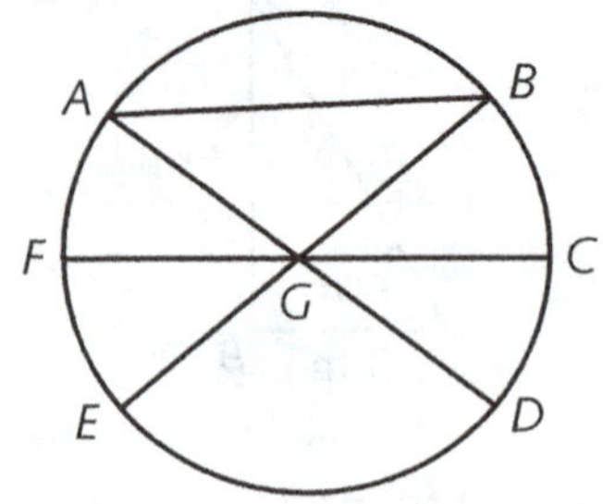

13 Which line segment could only be described as a chord?

A $\overline{EB}$

B $\overline{FC}$

C $\overline{AB}$

D $\overline{AD}$

14 Which term best describes $\overline{FC}$?

F radius

G line segment

H chord

J diameter

15 If the diameter is 8 inches, what is the radius?

A 12 in.

B 16 in.

C 2 in.

D 4 in.

16 Which line segment is a radius of the circle?

F $\overline{AD}$

G $\overline{EG}$

H $\overline{BE}$

J $\overline{AB}$

Review

17 What is the perimeter of this figure?

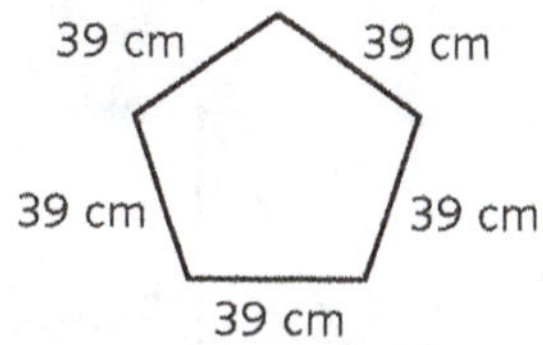

A 1,521 cm
B 156 cm
C 195 cm
D 312 cm

18 How many faces does this shape have?

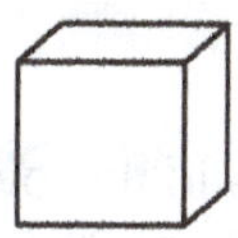

F three
G six
H eight
J nine

19 Which figure has no line of symmetry?

A 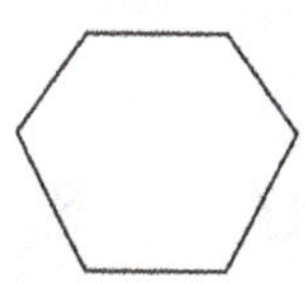

B 

C 

D 

20 Melody has a shower curtain that is 6 feet long. If she cuts 3 inches off the bottom, how long will it be?

F 75 in.
G 57 in.
H 69 in.
J 81 in.

21 100 grams _______ 1 kilogram

A $<$
B $>$
C $=$
D $\approx$

22 Which figure shows a cylinder?

F 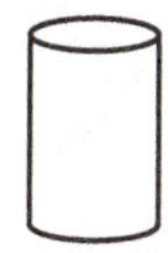

G 

H 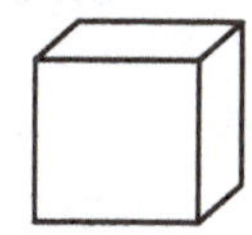

J 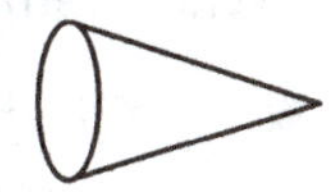

23 How many lines of symmetry does this figure have?

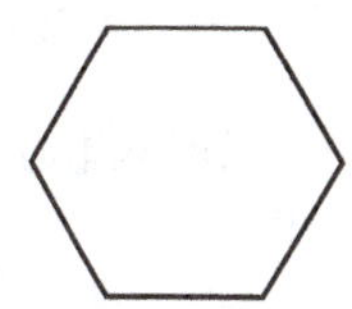

A none
B 1
C 2
D more than 2

24 What is the surface area of this figure?

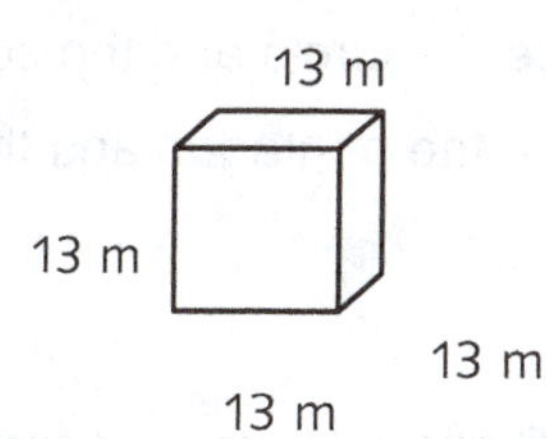

F 2,197 m^2
G 1,014 m^2
H 39 m^2
J 78 m^2

25 Marta bought 24 boxes of cereal, each weighing 420 grams. What is the total weight of the cereal she purchased?

A 100.08 cg
B 10.08 mg
C 10.08 kg
D 100.08 kg

26 Which term best describes this figure?

F line segment
G ray
H line
J point

27 Which best describes the position of point *S*?

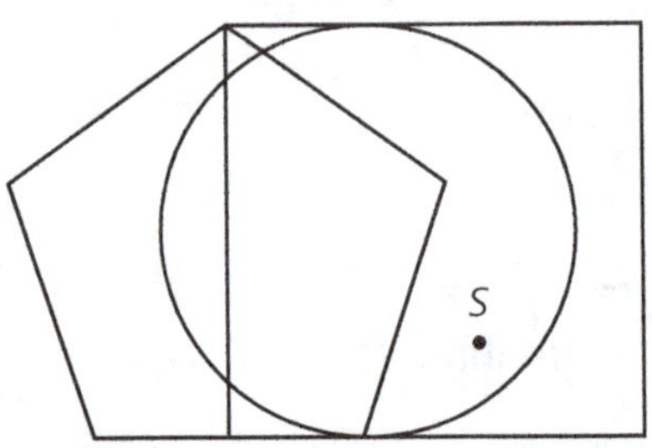

A inside the pentagon and the circle
B inside all three figures
C inside the circle and the square
D inside the pentagon and the square

28 Lines *AB* and *CD* are perpendicular. The angles formed by these lines are ______.

F right
G acute
H obtuse
J straight

29 What is the sum of $\angle ABC$, $\angle BCA$ and $\angle CAB$?

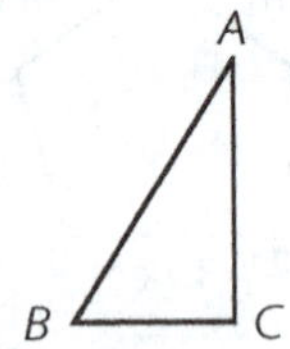

A 60°
B 90°
C 180°
D 360°

30 Tanya put a pie in the oven at 7:40 P.M., and it was ready at 8:35 P.M. How long did the pie take to bake?

F 45 min.
G 35 min.
H 65 min.
J 55 min.

31 Which angle is obtuse?

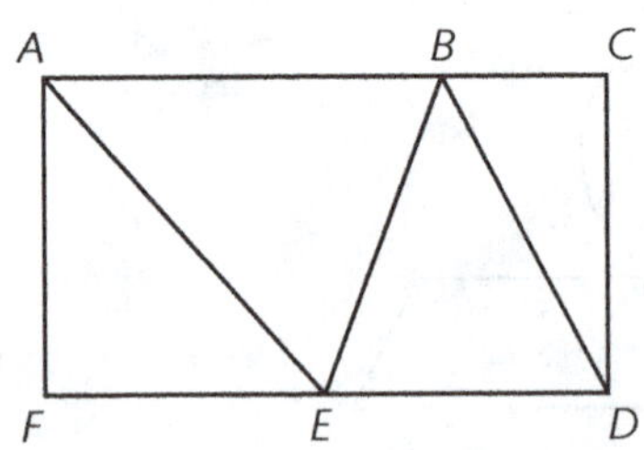

A $\angle AFE$
B $\angle BED$
C $\angle FEB$
D $\angle BDC$

32 Which measurement is equal to 2 gallons?

F 8 qt.
G 4 pt.
H 16 c.
J 32 fl. oz.

Answer Key

Page 3

1. $\frac{1}{2}$ lb.; $\frac{1}{4}$ c.; 2°F
2. 1 psi; 50 mL; 1°
3. $\frac{1}{4}$ c.; $\frac{3}{4}$ c.
4. $\frac{1}{2}$ in., $7\frac{1}{2}$ in.
5. 1°; 48° *or* 132°
6. 1 lb.; 128 lb.

Page 4

1. 3 in.
2. $2\frac{3}{4}$ in.
3. 4 in.
4. $3\frac{1}{2}$ in.
5. $1\frac{1}{2}$ in.
6. $2\frac{1}{4}$ in.
7. $2\frac{1}{2}$ in.
8. $1\frac{3}{4}$ in.
9. 2 in.
10. $\frac{3}{4}$ in.
11. $1\frac{1}{4}$ in.
12. $\frac{1}{2}$ in.
13. 1 in.
14. $\frac{1}{4}$ in.

15–24.

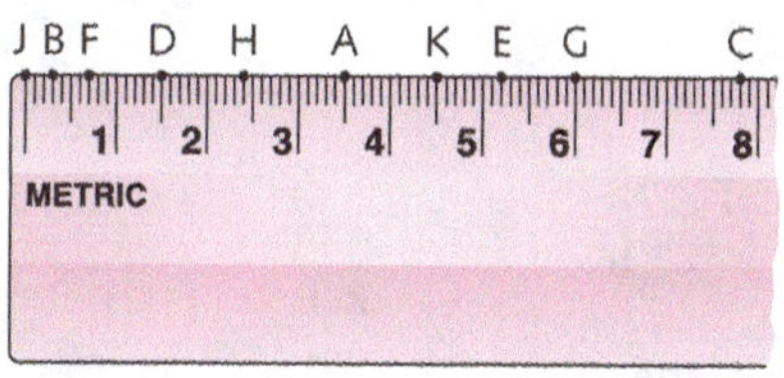

Page 5

1. ft. and in.
2. yd.
3. °F
4. lb.
5. gal.
6. yr.
7. tons
8. mi.
9. c. *or* pt. *or* oz.
10. °F
11. lb.
12. hr. and/or min.
13. gal.
14. oz.
15. c. *or* oz.
16. 104°F
17. 10 oz.
18. 10 lb.
19. 30 in.
20. 10 yd.
21. 1 gal.
22. 4 mo.
23. 2 lb.
24. 1 oz.
25. 35°F

Page 6

1. 7 ft.; 336 hr.; 256 oz.; 3 pt.
2. 60 ft.; 2 lb.; $2\frac{1}{4}$ hr.; 2 yd.
3. 2 mi.; 7.5 lb.; 4 min.; 1,320 ft.
4. 4 c.; 6 qt.
5. 48 hr.; 240 min.
6. 183 ft.; 564 in.
7. 144 in.; 8 ft.
8. 272 oz.; 8 lb.
9. 21 days; 140 min.
10. 8 pt.; 28 qt.

Page 6 continued

11. 3,520 yd.; 1 mi.
12. 28,800 sec.; 10 hr. 54 min.
13. 7,400 lb.; 45 lb. 3 oz.

Page 7

1. 12 ft. 3 in.; 12 ft. 1 in.; 14 min. 14 sec.; 2 hr. 5 min.
2. 14 yr. 2 mo.; 26 gal. 1 qt.; 72 ft. 3 in.; 14 yd. 1 ft.
3. 32 lb. 1 oz.; 5 lb.; 10 yd.; 54 lb. 2 oz.
4. 21 tons; 33 c. 4 oz.; 61 gal. 2 qt.; 22 min. 5 sec.
5. 1 ft. 4 in.; 11 ft. 10 in.; 15 min. 53 sec.; 43 min.
6. 8 ft. 10 in.; 15 ft. 7 in.; 1 gal. 1 qt.; 47 yr. 9 mo.
7. 3 lb. 6 oz.; 22 hr. 33 min.; 36 yd. 2 ft.; 10 tons 1,250 lb.
8. 4 gal. 2 qt.; 36 qt. 1 pt.; 21 pt. 1 c.; 1 c. 4 fl. oz.

Page 8

1. kilometer
2. kilogram
3. milliliter
4. meter
5. centimeter
6. milligram
7. liter
8. kilometer
9. centimeter
10. milliliter
11. >; =; >
12. <; >; <
13. >; <; >
14. =; =; =
15. =; <; =
16. >; >; <
17. >; <; >
18. =; >; =

Page 9

1. 8:15 A.M.
2. 3:30 P.M.
3. 3:45 P.M.
4. 20 min.
5. 2:30 A.M.
6. 10:45 A.M.
7. 45 min.
8. 1 hr. 45 min.
9. 19 min.
10. 2 hr. 22 min.

Page 10

1. line segment; ray; line; point
2. ray; line segment; point; line
3.

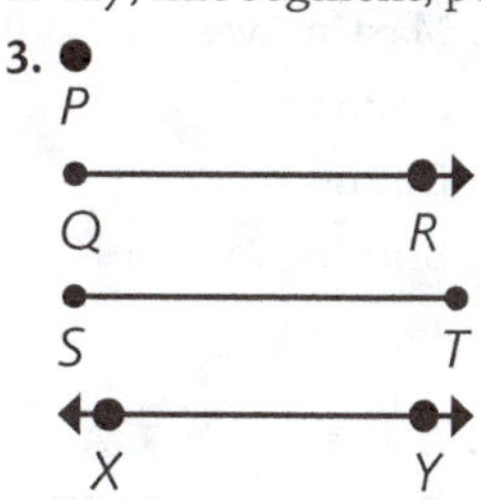

4.

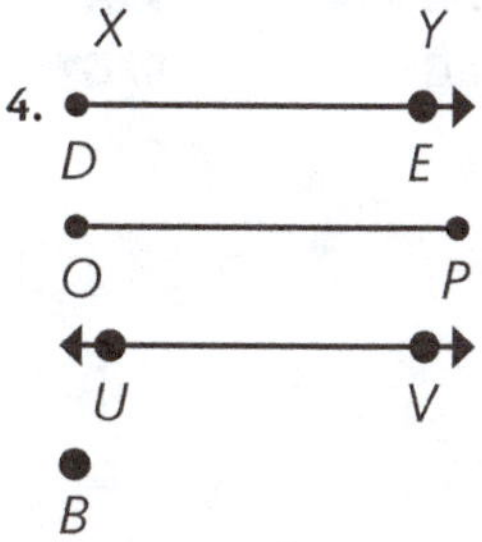

5. two
6. $\overline{AB}$ *or* $\overline{BA}$
7. $\overleftrightarrow{CD}$ *or* $\overleftrightarrow{DC}$
8. *F*

Answer Key

Page 11

1. right; obtuse; acute; acute

2. straight; obtuse; acute; right

Sample answers

3.

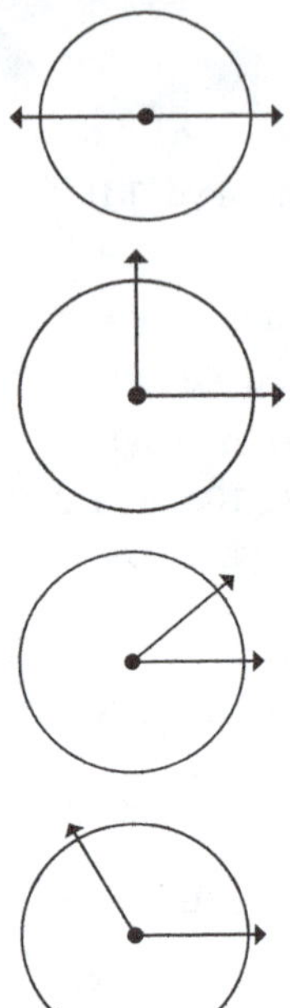

4–8.

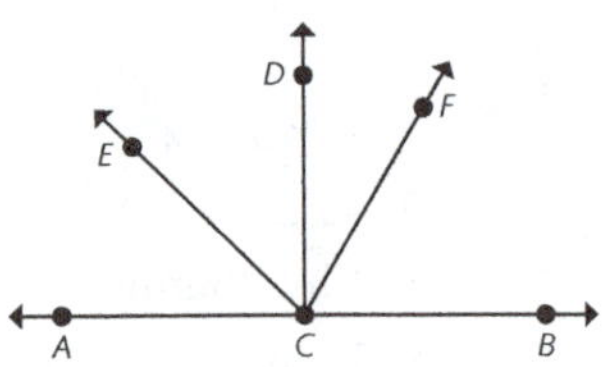

Page 12

1. C
2. F
3. C
4. G
5. intersecting
6. parallel
7. perpendicular
8. intersecting
9. perpendicular
10. intersecting
11. Martin Ave.
12. E 52nd St.
13. E 52nd St.
14. Bruning Ave.

Page 13

1. D
2. H
3. B
4. J
5. A
6. G
7. A
8. G

Page 14

1. D **2.** H **3.** D **4.** J

Sample answers

5. 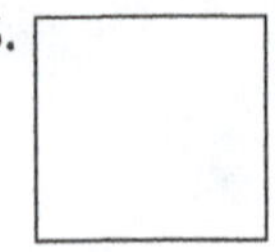 square

6. 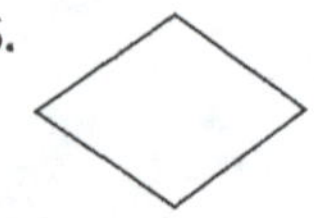 rhombus

7.  rectangle

8. 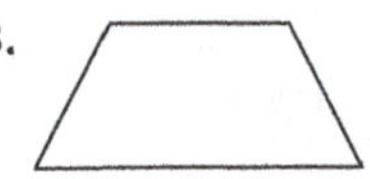 trapezoid

Page 15

1. C; A; B; A
2. 30°; right; scalene
3. 90°; right; scalene
4. 60°; acute; equilateral
5. 120°; obtuse; isosceles
6. F
7. F
8. T
9. F
10. T
11. T

Page 16

1. 22 in.; 42 m; 20 cm
2. 36 ft.; 25 ft.; 18 cm
3. 11 yd.; 48 km; 77 cm
4. 454 mm; 890 in.; 894 mi.
5. 9 m
6. 6 in.
7. 12 ft.
8. 30 cm, 32 cm, 30 cm, 32 cm

Page 17

1. 55 m^2; 65 ft.^{2}; 256 cm^2
2. 216 mi.^{2}; 1,225 yd.^{2}; 126 in.^{2}
3. 128 km^2; 430 yd.^{2}; 216 cm^2
4. 320 ft.^{2}
5. 12 ft.
6. 256 ft.^{2}
7. 2,592 in.^{2} *or* 18 ft.^{2}

Answer Key

Page 18

1. $\overline{FB}$ *or* $\overline{EA}$
2. $\overline{CD}$, $\overline{ED}$, *or* $\overline{AD}$
3. $\overline{EA}$
4. 170 mm
5. 198 in.
6. 492 km
7. 288 cm
8. 324 ft.
9. 116 m

10–12. *Sample answers*

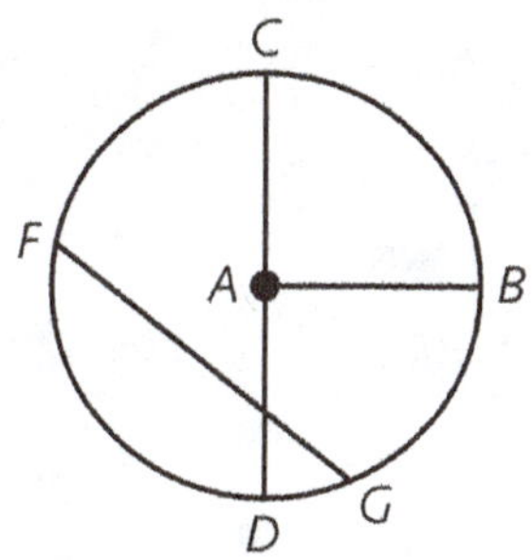

Page 19

1. rectangle; circle; circle
2. rectangle; square; triangle

3. B **4.** F **5.** A **6.** H

Page 20

Sample answers

1. 

2. 

3. 

4. 

5. 

6. 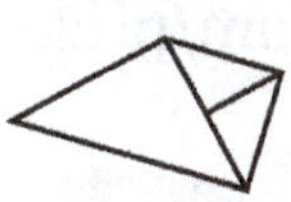

7. 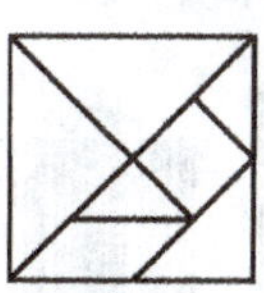

8. D

9. F

Page 21

1. A and D
2. B
3. A and B

4. 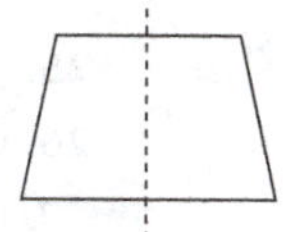

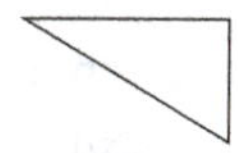

none

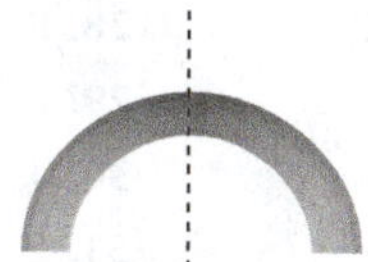

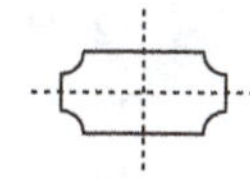

5. 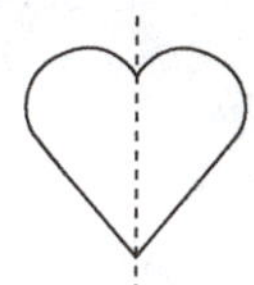

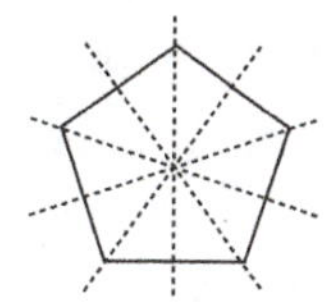

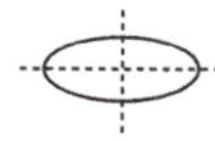

none

6. one; none; one; more than one

7. more than one; one; none; none

Page 22

1. similar; congruent; unlike
2. unlike; congruent; similar
3. similar; similar; congruent
4. unlike; unlike; similar
5. similar; unlike; congruent
6. congruent; unlike; congruent
7. *H*
8. *A*
9. *B*
10. unlike

Page 23

1. six **3.** five **5.** four

2. five **4.** eight **6.** six

7. 216 in.^{2}; 486 ft.^{2}; 3,456 m^2

8. 290 in.^{2}; 928 m^2; 478 ft.^{2}

Sample answers for 9–12

9. candle, column or pillar, tube-shaped mailer, can

10. fish tank, dresser, book, refrigerator

11. dice, ice cube, sugar cube, building blocks

12. ice cream cone, clown hat, witch hat, funnel

Answer Key

Page 24

1. D	**3.** D	**5.** C	**7.** B
2. G	**4.** H	**6.** G	**8.** F

Pages 25–28, Review

1. A	**9.** D	**17.** C	**25.** C
2. G	**10.** J	**18.** G	**26.** G
3. A	**11.** B	**19.** C	**27.** C
4. H	**12.** H	**20.** H	**28.** F
5. C	**13.** C	**21.** A	**29.** C
6. J	**14.** J	**22.** F	**30.** J
7. B	**15.** D	**23.** D	**31.** C
8. G	**16.** G	**24.** G	**32.** F

mheducation.com/prek-12

McGraw Hill Education

MHID 0-07-658624-3
978-0-07-658624-0
EAN
9 780076 586240
99701